WriteShop
Junior

Fold-N-Go Grammar Pack

by Nancy I. Sanders

WriteShop Junior Level 2 Fold-N-Go Grammar Pack
© 2014 by Nancy I. Sanders.
Published and distributed by Demme Learning.

This material is to be used in conjunction with WriteShop Junior Book E Teacher's Guide.

All rights reserved. No part of this book may be reproduced, stored in a retrieval system, or transmitted in any form by any means—electronic, mechanical, photocopying, recording, or otherwise—without prior written permission from Demme Learning.

writeshop.com

1-888-854-6284 or +1 717-283-1448 | demmelearning.com
Lancaster, Pennsylvania USA

ISBN 978-1-60826-664-7
Revision Code 0122

Printed in the United States of America by The P.A. Hutchison Company
 2 3 4 5 6 7 8 9 10

For information regarding CPSIA on this printed material call: 1-888-854-6284
and provide reference #0122-01142022

Fold-N-Go Grammar

Introduction

Though *Fold-N-Go Grammar*® is not a complete grammar curriculum, you may find that it helps your child acquire many grammar skills he needs to write successfully at this level. If so, by all means use the guides as your main resource for teaching grammar skills. However, if he struggles to learn the rules about punctuation, sentence structure, or other writing skills, use *Fold-N-Go Grammar* to supplement a more complete grammar program.

Fold-N-Go Grammar is a required component of WriteShop Junior. Even if you are not teaching WriteShop Junior, you can still use *Fold-N-Go Grammar* as an independent resource. Either way, each *Fold-N-Go* helps review or introduce key grammar and writing rules in a fun and engaging way.

Level 2 Fold-N-Go Grammar Pack - Contents

Make the *Fold-N-Go*

Complete the Activities

Store the *Fold-N-Go*

Grammar Lessons

    Lesson 1   Sentences

    Lesson 2   Four Kinds of Sentences

    Lesson 3   Compound Sentences

    Lesson 4   Parts of Speech: Review

    Lesson 5   Dialogue

    Lesson 6   Homophones, Homonyms, and Homographs

    Lesson 7   Five Paragraphs

    Lesson 8   Prefixes and Suffixes

    Lesson 9   Compound Words

    Lesson 10   Synonyms and Antonyms

Answer Keys

Make the Fold-N-Go

This pack will produce 10 unique *Fold-N-Go* grammar guides, six pages each. The pages are designed to be stapled together and affixed inside a file folder to form a large flipbook. If you're teaching more than one child, make one for each student.

Each *Fold-N-Go* is assembled in exactly the same way. Put them together yourself or enlist your child's help.

Gather Supplies

- 10 letter-size manila or colored file folders or a set of 10 fancy file folders.
- Stapler
- Clear packing tape and clear circle stickers (optional)

Prepare the Pages

1. From the Level 2 Fold-N-Go Grammar Pack, remove the six pages for the current lesson's *Fold-N-Go*.
2. Identify the correct page number of each page as shown (figure 1).

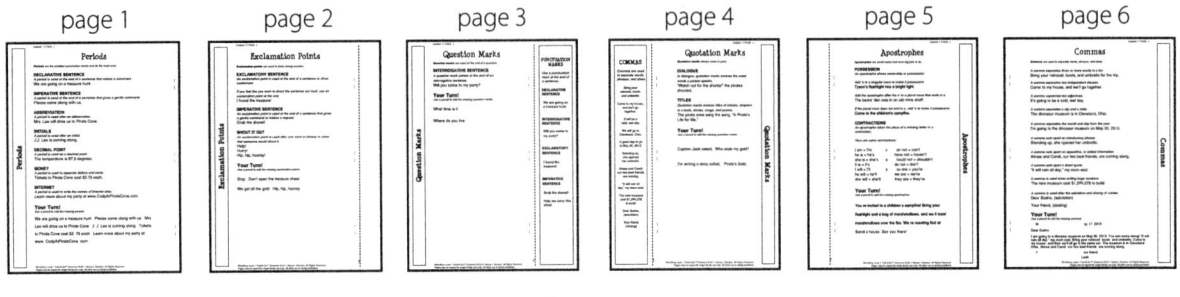

figure 1

3. Cut along the dotted lines on pages 2 and 5 (figure 2).
4. Cut along the dotted lines on pages 3 and 4 as shown (figure 3).
5. Trim the two bookmarks and laminate if desired (figure 4).

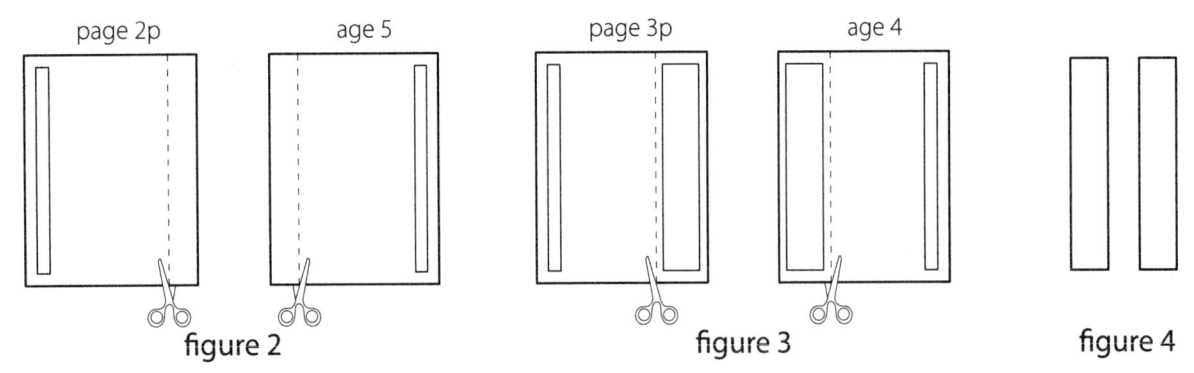

figure 2   **figure 3**   **figure 4**

Assemble the Fold-N-Go

1. Stack pages 1, 2, and 3 as shown so that their right edges align together. The left edges should be offset from each other and clearly show the titles of each page (figure 5). Staple them together along the right edges with three staples as shown (figure 6).
2. Stack pages 4, 5, and 6 as shown so that their left edges

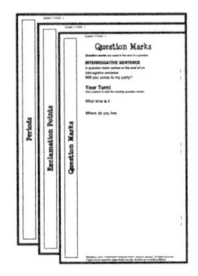

figure 5   **figure 6**

align together. The right edges should be offset from each other and clearly show the titles of each page (figure 7). Staple them together along the left edges with three staples as shown (figure 8).

3. Staple the stack of pages 1, 2, and 3 to the left side of the inside of the file folder along the top and bottom of page 1 as shown (figure 9). Do not staple all three pages. Only page 1 will be stapled to the folder. Alternatively, you may tape or glue page 1 in place.

4. Staple the stack of pages 4, 5, and 6 to the right side of the inside of the file folder along the top and bottom of page 6 as shown (figure 10). Do not staple all three pages. Only page 6 will be stapled to the folder. Alternatively, you may tape or glue page 6 in place.

5. For durability, tape a strip of clear packing tape down the center of the file folder to cover the staples (figure 11). On the outside, affix a clear circle sticker over each staple to avoid scratching or catching on clothes (figure 12).

6. On both the tab and front of the folder, write the name of the *Fold-N-Go*. Let your child decorate the cover, if desired.

Make the Bookmarks

Along with each *Fold-N-Go* grammar guide, you will cut out two bookmarks that highlight the lesson's grammar or writing skills at a glance.

1. For durability, laminate the bookmarks or glue them on cardstock. Consider gluing or laminating them back-to-back to form one bookmark for each writing skill.

2. Store these in a jar in the writing center. Keep them handy so your child can pull the bookmarks out and refresh his memory about grammar rules during writing or editing.

3. You may also choose to tape or glue these inside a file folder as a quick reference. Use one file folder to store bookmarks from Lessons 1-5 and another to store bookmarks from Lessons 6-10. Label the covers and tabs accordingly (figure 13).

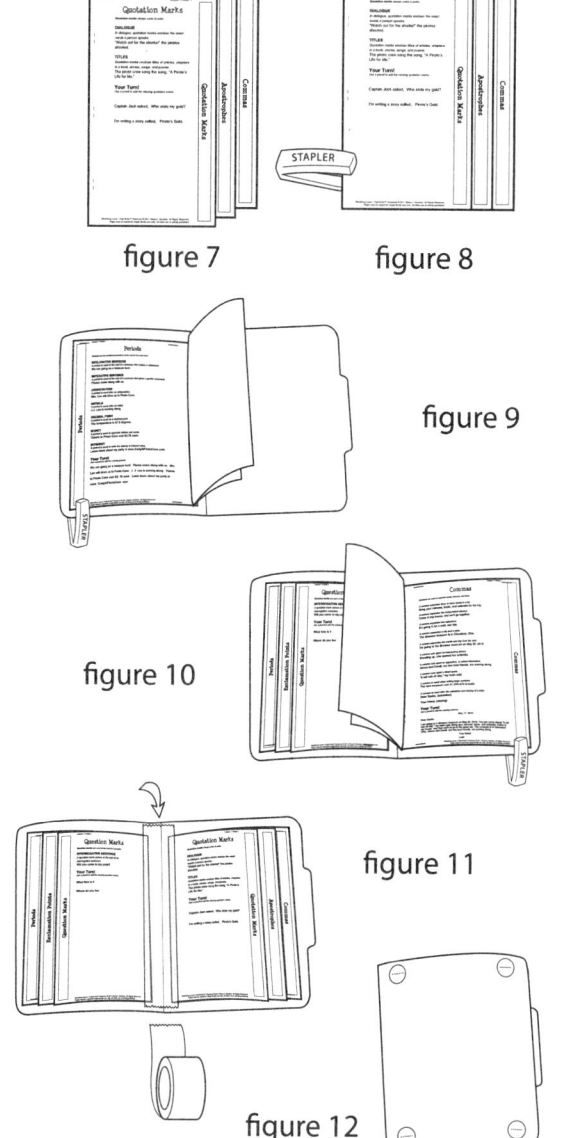

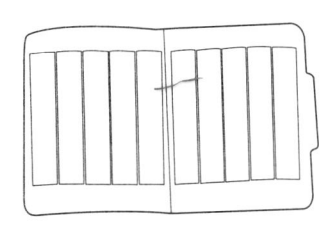

figure 7

figure 8

figure 9

figure 10

figure 11

figure 12

figure 13

Complete the Activities

When to Do Fold-N-Go Activities

WriteShop Junior Students: If you are using WriteShop Junior Book E, each lesson will instruct you to assemble and complete a new *Fold-N-Go* together with your child. Because most *Fold-N-Gos* are directly related to their corresponding lessons, your child will benefit from making and using each one as it is assigned (see Book E Teacher's Guide). Even if he is eager and enthusiastic, it's best to keep your child on schedule and not let him jump ahead to the other *Fold-N-Gos* until they are assigned.

All Other Students: If you are using the Level 2 Fold-N-Go Grammar Pack as a stand-alone grammar resource, feel free to work at your own pace. Or, make one *Fold-N-Go* every week for 10 weeks according to this schedule:

Day 1: Assemble the *Fold-N-Go*

Day 2: Pages 1 and 2

Day 3: Pages 3 and 4

Day 4: Pages 5 and 6

How to Do Fold-N-Go Activities

1. Open the *Fold-N-Go* so you and your student can easily see all six pages at a glance.

2. Read through each page together, allowing time for your child to complete the pencil activities. Do not let him use a pen for these exercises.

3. After each pencil activity, discuss his answers. (An answer key is provided in the back of the Level 2 Fold-N-Go Grammar Pack.)

4. If he makes a mistake, praise him for his efforts. Offer gentle correction and erase the mistake or help him use correction tape before having him write the correct answer.

5. Because this guide will be used in future lessons as a point of reference, it's important to answer each pencil activity correctly. As an option, your child may dictate the correct answer for you to write down. When finished, check your child's responses against the Answer Key in the back of the Fold-N-Go Grammar Pack. If the material is new to him and it was a challenge to learn, plan on re-teaching this topic and practicing this skill during future sessions.

Store the Fold-N-Go

One of the purposes of *Fold-N-Go Grammar* is to create a handy resource for your child to refer to during the writing and editing process. Therefore, keep each folder easily accessible in your writing area. Here are some storage suggestions.

- File drawer in your child's desk
- 3.5-inch accordion-style letter-size file pocket
- File box for holding letter-size file folders

Lesson 1 Sentences | PAGE 1

Simple Subject

A sentence is a group of words that tells a complete thought.
Every sentence starts with a capital letter.
Every sentence ends with punctuation.
Every sentence has a subject and a predicate.

Subject
The subject is the noun or pronoun that the sentence is all about.

A **knight** trotted through the forest on his horse.

He whistled a happy tune.

Simple Subject
*A simple subject is **one** noun or pronoun that the sentence is all about.*

The **horse** galloped toward the castle.

DID YOU KNOW?
There can be many nouns or pronouns in a sentence, but the subject is always the star of the show!

Your Turn!
Draw a star above the simple subject in these sentences.

The knight rode his horse up to the castle.

He trotted across the drawbridge on his mighty steed.

They crossed over the murky moat.

The princess saw the knight approaching the castle.

She waved a colorful pennant!

Complete Subject

*A **complete subject** is the noun and the words with it that describe the noun.*

The clever princess shot an arrow.

The chivalrous knight cheered.

His gallant steed stomped its foot.

DID YOU KNOW?
A simple subject is just the noun or pronoun.

The **princess** shot an arrow.

It sailed through the air.

DID YOU KNOW?
If you have a hard time finding the subject in a sentence, first find the verb. Then ask "who" or "what" is doing the verb action.

The young princess shot an arrow.

   The verb is **shot**.
   Who shot the arrow?
   The **young princess**.

Your Turn!
Circle the complete subject in each sentence.

The lovely princess aimed at the moat.

Her sharp arrow got stuck in a tree trunk!

The sleek horse trotted over to the oak tree.

The strong, muscular knight pulled out the arrow.

Simple Predicate

The simple predicate is the one verb that shows what the subject is doing.

A fire-breathing dragon **flew** above the castle.

The princess **screamed**!

DID YOU KNOW?
A verb can show action or a state of being.

Action: The dragon **landed** near the castle.

State of being: The knight **was** ready to fight the dragon.

Your Turn!
Circle the simple predicate in these sentences.

The knight drew his sword.

The princess shut her eyes tightly.

The dragon flapped his leathery wings.

He was a friendly dragon!

He came to the castle for his birthday.

Sentences

A sentence is a group of words that tells a complete thought.

DID YOU KNOW?
Every sentence starts with a capital letter.

Every sentence ends with punctuation.

Every sentence has a subject and a predicate.

SUBJECT
The subject is the noun or pronoun that the sentence is all about.

The **dragon** breathes fire.

PREDICATE
The predicate is the verb that shows what the subject is doing.

The dragon **breathes** fire.

Lesson I Sentences I PAGE 4

Sentences

SIMPLE SUBJECT

The **dragon** flew to the castle.

COMPLETE SUBJECT

The fire-breathing dragon flew to the castle.

COMPOUND SUBJECT

The **dragon** and the **knight** flew to the castle.

SIMPLE PREDICATE

The princess **practiced** her archery lessons.

COMPLETE PREDICATE

The princess **practiced her archery lessons.**

COMPOUND PREDICATE

The princess **shot** an arrow, **hit** the target, and **won** the tournament.

Complete Predicate

A complete predicate is the verb and the words with it that describe the verb.

Everyone **sang "Happy Birthday."**

The dragon **opened his presents**.

He **got a new barbeque**!

DID YOU KNOW?
A simple predicate is just the verb in the sentence.

The guests **sang**.

A complete predicate is the verb and the words with it that describe it.

The guests **sang to the dragon**.

Your Turn!
Match each of these subjects with a complete predicate to form a sentence. Draw a line from the subject to the complete predicate of your choice.

Subject	Complete Predicate
Queen Hildegard	blew bubbles in the air.
Princess Camille	scratched his head.
King George	toasted gooey marshmallows for s'mores.
Knight Aaron the Stouthearted	tripped over the royal carpet.
Felix the Dragon	laughed at the jester.

Complete Predicate

Lesson I Sentences I PAGE 5

Compound Subject

A compound subject occurs when two or more simple subjects (nouns) share the same predicate (verb).
The simple subjects are usually connected by the word "and."

The **princess** and the **dragon** are friends.

Now the **knight** and the **dragon** are friends, too.

The **knight** and the **princess** gave presents to the dragon at his birthday party.

DID YOU KNOW?
In a compound subject, all the nouns or pronouns in the subject use the same verb.

The knight and the princess baked a cake for the dragon.

Compound Subject: knight, princess
Verb: baked

The knight, princess, king, and queen baked a cake for the dragon.

Compound Subject: knight, princess, king, queen
Verb: baked

Your Turn!
Underline the compound subject in the sentence. Then complete the maze that leads to the cake. Only one castle entrance will work! (Hint: Start with the picture of the correct compound subject.)

The knight and the princess performed a juggling show for the dragon, the king, and the queen.

Compound Subject

Compound Predicate

When one noun or pronoun has two or more verbs, it has a compound predicate. A compound predicate is when a subject (noun) has two or more simple predicates (verbs).

The party guests **arrived** at the castle and **carried** presents inside.

After the birthday party, Felix the Dragon **flew** home and **wrote** a thank-you letter to his friends.

DID YOU KNOW?
In a compound predicate, one subject is performing all the actions.

Felix the Dragon **played** with his new remote-control fire engine, **rode** his new scooter, and **toasted** marshmallows on his new barbecue.

Your Turn!
Underline the compound predicates in these sentences. Then find and circle these compound predicates in the word search below.

Princess Camille shot an arrow, hit the target, and won the tournament.

Knight Aaron the Stouthearted trotted, galloped, and raced his horse to the finish line.

Felix the fire-breathing dragon clapped and cheered for his friends.

```
R Q C W T O H S X
A G A L L O P E D
C Q V W A X W G T
E Z O A Q P H A I
D N L V H Z P L H
A C T R O T T E D
R A C H E E R E D
```

Declarative Sentence

LET'S REVIEW!
A sentence is a group of words that tells a complete thought.
Every sentence starts with a capital letter.
Every sentence ends with punctuation.
Every sentence has a subject and a predicate.

DID YOU KNOW?
There are four kinds of sentences:

declarative
interrogative
imperative
exclamatory

DECLARATIVE
A declarative sentence tells a statement.

Adventure Park is a place where kids can play in a giant mud pit, build things out of boards, and climb rock walls.

Tori wants to go to Adventure Park.

She will ask Levi to come along.

DID YOU KNOW?
A declarative sentence ends with a period.

Your Turn!
Circle the correct punctuation so that each example is a declarative sentence.

Tori picked up the phone   .   !   ?

She called her friend, Levi   !   ?   .

Tori asked Levi to go to Adventure Park   ?   .   !

Interrogative Sentence

*An **interrogative** sentence asks a question.*

What time did Tori and Levi go to Adventure Park?

Did they play in the mud or build a fort first?

DID YOU KNOW?
An interrogative sentence ends with a question mark.

Your Turn!
Add correct ending punctuation to each of these sentences. Underline the interrogative sentences.

What does Levi like to do the most at Adventure Park

He likes to play in the slimy mud pit

What is Tori's favorite thing to do at Adventure Park

She likes to get a hammer and nails and build a fort

Which one would you like to do the most

Imperative Sentence

*An **imperative** sentence states a command.*

Levi, please put your shoes in the locker.
Tori, carry the nails in a bucket.

DID YOU KNOW?
Sometimes the subject in an imperative sentence is not written down. The unwritten subject is "you."

Bring a hammer. = (You) Bring a hammer.
Bring a board to build the fort. = (You) Bring a board to build the fort.

Your Turn!
Change these sentences into imperative sentences. Write the new sentences on the blank lines.

I would like you to wash the mud off your feet, please.

_____

_____

It would be nice if you would pound the nail harder.

_____

_____

Tori needs you to bring her a water bottle.

_____

_____

Sentences

DID YOU KNOW?
There are four kinds of sentences:

declarative
interrogative
imperative
exclamatory

DECLARATIVE
A declarative sentence tells a statement.

INTERROGATIVE
An interrogative sentence asks a question.

IMPERATIVE
An imperative sentence states a command.

EXCLAMATORY
An exclamatory sentence shows a lot of feeling.

Sentences

A sentence is a group of words that tells a complete thought.

Every sentence starts with a capital letter.

Every sentence ends with punctuation.

Every sentence has a subject and a predicate.

FRAGMENTS

A fragment is a group of words that does NOT tell a complete thought.

RUN-ONS

Run-on sentences have too much information and are too long.

Lesson 2 Four Sentences | PAGE 4

Exclamatory Sentence

*An **exclamatory** sentence shows a lot of feeling.*

Levi loves playing in the mud!
Tori thinks a day at Adventure Park is the best!

DID YOU KNOW?
An exclamatory sentence ends with an exclamation mark.

Your Turn!
Change these declarative sentences into exclamatory sentences. Then write your own exclamatory sentence on the blank lines.

Tori and Levi wanted to play in the mud all day.

They had never been so muddy.

Levi built the tallest fort ever.

They had tons of fun.

_____

_____

_____

_____

Exclamatory Sentence

Sentence Fragments

*Sentence **fragments** are not sentences at all!*
A fragment is a group of words that does NOT tell a complete thought.

DID YOU KNOW?
A fragment might be missing a subject.
A fragment might be missing a predicate.
A fragment might be missing both a subject and a predicate.

Examples of Fragments
Tori's friend, Levi
The muddy swamp at Adventure Park
Hammers and nails
sloshed in the mud
climbed the rock wall

Your Turn!
Each letter in this cryptogram stands for a different letter. Fill in the blank above each letter with the letter you think it stands for, using the clues in the blanks that have already been filled in. When you fill in all the blanks, you can read the secret message! The secret message will help you spot the difference between a fragment and a sentence.

_ _ _ _ Y   _ _ _ _ _ E _ _
J C J D Z   L J E P J E T J

_ _ S _   _ _ _ _ _ _ T
W Q L Q   L G N S J T P

_ _ _   _
Q E M   Q

_ _ _ _ _ C _ _ _ .
F D J M B T Q P J

(Secret message: EVERY SENTENCE HAS A SUBJECT AND A PREDICATE.)

Run-on Sentences

Run-on *sentences have too much information and are too long.*

Tori and Levi had so much fun at Adventure Park because they got to stay all day but even though they wanted to climb the rock wall they didn't really have time to go there because first they spent a long time splashing in the slimy mud pit and then they decided to go build a fort together and by then it was time to go home.

DID YOU KNOW?
You can fix a run-on sentence. It's easy! Just divide a run-on sentence into two or more shorter sentences. Then cross out the extra words you don't need.

Tori and Levi had so much fun at Adventure Park. ~~because~~ They got to stay all day. ~~but~~ Even though they wanted to climb the rock wall, they didn't really have time to go there. ~~because~~ First they spent a long time splashing in the slimy mud pit. ~~and~~ Then they decided to go build a fort together. ~~and~~ By then it was time to go home.

Your Turn!
Fix this run-on sentence. Divide it up into at least three shorter sentences. Cross out the extra words you don't need.

On the way home, Tori asked Levi what he liked most about Adventure Park and he said he used to like the mud pit the best but not anymore because he had so much fun building the fort with Tori that now he liked that part the best and then Levi asked Tori about her favorite part.

Compound Sentences

*When two sentences are joined together to make one sentence, it is a **compound sentence**.*

SENTENCE #1
Emma lives in Alaska.

SENTENCE #2
She has a husky named Ollie.

COMPOUND SENTENCE
Emma lives in Alaska, and she has a husky named Ollie.

Your Turn!
Underline the two sentences in each of the following compound sentences. The first one has been done for you.

<u>Emma's family went on a camping trip</u>, and <u>her cousin Nick came with them</u>.

Ollie wanted to go along, so they brought him, too.

They saw caribou, but the caribou galloped away.

Soon they found a place to camp, and they put up their tent.

The cousins felt safe, for they didn't see any polar bears.

Two Sentences

*A compound sentence is made up of **two sentences**.*

<u>Emma ran across the tundra</u>, and <u>Nick ran after her</u>.
<u>Ollie followed Nick</u>, and <u>a polar bear chased them all</u>!

DID YOU KNOW?
A sentence has a subject and a predicate. If it's missing a subject or a predicate, it's not a sentence at all. It's a fragment.

IDENTIFY A COMPOUND SENTENCE
To identify a compound sentence, first find the two sentences. "Ollie stopped running, so the polar bear stopped running, too."

Step 1: Look for the subject and predicate in the first sentence.

Step 2: Then look for the subject and predicate in the second sentence.

First sentence:
Ollie stopped running.
Subject: Ollie
Predicate: stopped

Second sentence:
The polar bear stopped running, too.
Subject: bear
Predicate: stopped

Your Turn!
Underline the sentences. Put an X on the fragments. Then draw a line from a sentence on the left to a sentence on the right to make compound sentences.

The polar bear danced,	and he sang a silly song.
Emma's parka and boots,	for all the animals danced.
A caribou joined them,	so Ollie danced, too!
Nick twirled in a circle,	and an igloo and sleds.
It was the best Arctic party,	but he didn't sing.

Two Sentences

Lesson 3 Compound Sentences and Conjunctions | PAGE 2

Conjunctions

*The little words that join two sentences together in a compound sentence are called **conjunctions**.*

DID YOU KNOW?
*There are seven common conjunctions used in compound sentences. These are known as **FANBOYS**. That's an acronym spelled from the first letter of each of these conjunctions:*

for
and
nor
but
or
yet
so

DID YOU KNOW?
A semicolon (;) can also be used as a conjunction in a compound sentence.

Emma and Nick went hiking; they looked for moss to help build a campfire.

Your Turn!
Circle the seven conjunctions listed above. Look forward, backward, up, down and diagonally.

```
X O R G J S D L
C V M W Q O B A
K H P F Z M Y N
T S L V R O F D
U Y W X R J H M
B M G O K P L C
Q X N N T E Y Z
```

Compound Sentence

*When two sentences are joined together to make one sentence, it is a **compound sentence**.*

SENTENCE #1
Emma lives in Alaska.

SENTENCE #2
She has a husky named Ollie.

COMPOUND SENTENCE
Emma lives in Alaska, and she has a husky named Ollie.

DID YOU KNOW?
A sentence has a subject and a predicate.

If it's missing a subject or a predicate, it's not a sentence at all. It's a fragment.

Conjunctions

There are seven common conjunctions used in compound sentences.

These are known as FANBOYS.

That's an acronym spelled from the first letter of each of these conjunctions:

for: *to explain why*

and: *to show relationship*

nor: *to show a double negative*

but: *to show something different*

or: *to show something else*

yet: *to show a contrast*

so: *to show a result*

DID YOU KNOW?
A semicolon (;) can also be used as a conjunction in a compound sentence.

Emma and Nick went hiking; they looked for moss to help build a campfire.

CHOOSING CONJUNCTIONS
When writing a compound sentence, choose your conjunction carefully. Each one can give a different meaning to your sentence.

Lesson 3 Compound Sentences and Conjunctions | PAGE 4

Commas

*In a compound sentence, the first sentence is followed by a **comma**.*

Emma paddled her kayak out to sea, and Nick followed her in his kayak.

AFTER THE COMMA
In a compound sentence, the conjunction comes after the comma.

A playful seal swam up to Emma, **and** it tipped over her kayak!

AFTER THE CONJUNCTION
In a compound sentence, the second sentence comes after the conjunction.

The seal tried to tip Nick's kayak, but **Nick tricked it**.

DID YOU KNOW?
*When conjunctions are used in compound sentences, they are sometimes called **linking words**.*

Your Turn!
*Put a comma in each compound sentence. Remember: The comma comes **after** the first sentence and **before** the conjunction.*

Nick helped Emma get in her kayak and they both went back to shore.

The seal followed them but Ollie started to bark.

The seal tossed a ball of moss to Ollie so Ollie played fetch.

Emma gave the seal a snack for it looked hungry.

Choosing Conjunctions

When writing a compound sentence, carefully choose which conjunction you want to use. Each one can give a different **meaning** *to your compound sentence.*

for: *Use this conjunction to explain why.*
The seal wanted to eat, **for** Ollie was chewing bones.

and: *Use this conjunction to show two related actions or events.*
The seal wanted to fetch, **and** Ollie wanted to play, too.

nor: *Use this conjunction to show a double negative.*
There weren't any sticks to play with, **nor** were there any balls to throw.

but: *Use this conjunction to show something different.*
The seal tossed a rock, **but** it hurt Ollie's teeth.

or: *Use this conjunction to show a different choice.*
They could play fetch, **or** they could swim in the sea.

yet: *Use this conjunction to show a contrast.*
Ollie could paddle, **yet** the seal could dive and glide!

so: *Use this conjunction to show a result.*
Ollie got cold and wet, **so** they swam back to shore.

Your Turn!
Write a conjunction on each blank line in the sentences below. Choose the conjunction that gives the sentence the correct meaning.

The seal performed a show, _____ Emma and Nick watched.

The seal clapped its fins, _____ it jumped over a kayak.

Emma and Nick whistled, _____ Ollie barked and howled.

Emma had five fish, _____ she gave them to the seal.

Sentence Length

*When you are writing, you can make your writing more interesting by including **sentences of different lengths**. Changing two short sentences into a compound sentence is a quick way to add a long sentence.*

TWO SHORT SENTENCES:
The villagers held a blanket toss.
Emma bounced up high.

ONE LONGER COMPOUND SENTENCE:
The villagers held a blanket toss, and Emma bounced up high.

DID YOU KNOW?
There are many different conjunctions, and they have many different jobs to do. The seven FANBOYS conjunctions are the ones used in compound sentences.

Your Turn!
All the sentences in this paragraph are nearly the same length. Make the paragraph more interesting. Change two sentences that are next to each other into one compound sentence. Then change two more sentences into another compound sentence. Write these two new compound sentences on the blank lines below.

    Emma loved the blanket toss. It was held every summer. All the villagers gathered. Everyone held tightly to a walrus skin. Emma was invited to go first. She stood on the walrus skin. Then she bounced. It was like being on a trampoline. Emma bounced high into the sky. It was so exciting!

_____

_____

_____

_____

Nouns: Review

Nouns are words that name a person, place, or thing.

Robo-Dog is a **dog** that is a **robot**.
Patti likes to play with **Robo-Dog**.

PROPER NOUNS
Proper nouns describe the name of a particular person, place, day of the week, month, or holiday.

Robo-Dog, Patti, Monday, Thanksgiving

COMMON NOUNS
Common nouns do not name a particular person, place, or thing.

dog, robot, doghouse, park, treat, toy

DID YOU KNOW?
Proper nouns always begin with a capital letter.

PLURAL NOUNS
A singular noun is one person, place, or thing.
When there are two or more, write the plural noun.

DID YOU KNOW?
There are rules for changing singular nouns into plural nouns.
Check the spelling of a plural noun in the dictionary.

Your Turn!
Write a list of nouns that name things or people you think Robo-Dog likes to play with. Choose some common nouns and some proper nouns.

_____   _____

_____   _____

_____   _____

_____

Verbs: Review

Verbs are words that show action or a state of being.

LINKING VERBS
Some verbs link the subject with more information about it. Linking verbs show a state of being.

Robo-Dog **is** smart.
Robo-Dog **likes** to play fetch.

ACTION VERBS
Most verbs show action.

Robo-Dog **rolls** over.
He **plays** dead.
He **sits** up and **begs** for a treat.

PAST TENSE REGULAR VERBS
Past tense shows action that happened in the past.

Robo-Dog **sat** up and **begged** for a treat.

PRESENT TENSE
Present tense shows action that happens right now, in the present.

Robo-Dog **sits** up and **begs** for a treat.

FUTURE TENSE
Future tense shows action that will happen later, in the future.

Robo-Dog **will sit** up. He **will beg** for a treat.

Your Turn!
Circle the verbs.

Robo-Dog walked with Patti to the store.

He will perform tricks for her friends.

He is the happiest robot dog in the world!

Pronouns: Review

Pronouns are words that take the place of nouns.

A CD player is inside Robo-Dog's body.
It is inside **his** body.

Robo-Dog plays CDs.
He plays **them**.

MALE OR FEMALE PRONOUNS
Some pronouns are male or female, just like the nouns they replace.

   Robo-Dog: he, him, his
   Patti: she, her, hers

SINGULAR OR PLURAL PRONOUNS
Some pronouns are singular and some are plural, just like the nouns they replace.

   Robo-Dog plays Patti's favorite CDs.
   He plays **them**.

PERSONAL PRONOUNS
A personal pronoun is used to replace the name of the person or people you are writing about.

   I, me, my, mine
   he, him, his
   she, her, hers
   it, its
   we, us, our, ours
   they, them, their, theirs
   you, your, yours

DID YOU KNOW?
There are many kinds of pronouns, but personal pronouns are the ones you use the most.

Your Turn!
Unscramble the letters and write the personal pronouns.

em = _____   rhe = _____

etyh = _____   oyu = _____

esh = _____   mnei = _____

Nouns
name a person, place, or thing.

PROPER NOUNS
name of a particular person, place, or thing.

Robo-Dog
Patti

COMMON NOUNS
do not name a particular person, place, or thing.

toy
treat

Verbs
show action or a state of being.

LINKING VERBS
show a state of being.

Robo-Dog **is** smart.

ACTION VERBS
Most verbs show action.

Robo-Dog **rolls** over.

Pronouns
replace a proper name

Adjectives: Review

Adjectives describe nouns and pronouns.

ADJECTIVES COME BEFORE
An adjective often comes right before the noun or pronoun it describes.

Robo-Dog has **real** fur.

ADJECTIVES COME AFTER
An adjective can also come after the noun or pronoun it describes.

If the sentence has a linking verb, the adjective often comes after the linking verb.

Robo-Dog's eyes are **electronic**.

ADJECTIVES COMPARE THINGS

ONE THING
Some adjectives describe one noun or pronoun.

Robo-Dog is a **smart** pet.

TWO THINGS
Some adjectives can be used to compare two nouns or pronouns.

Robo-Dog is **smarter** than Robo-Cat.
Robo-Dog is **smarter** than Robo-Snake.

THREE THINGS
Some adjectives can be used to compare three or more nouns or pronouns.

Robo-Dog is the **smartest** of the three pets.

Your Turn!
Circle the correct adjective.

Robo-Dog is **strong / stronger** than Robo-Cat.

Robo-Cat is **friendlier / friendliest** than Robo-Snake.

Robo-Snake is the **scarier / scariest** of all!

Adjectives
describe nouns and pronouns.

ADJECTIVES COME BEFORE
Robo-Dog has **real** fur.

ADJECTIVES COME AFTER
Robo-Dog's eyes are **electronic**.

ADJECTIVES COMPARE THINGS
Adjectives can compare nouns and pronouns.

Adverbs
describe verbs.

Robo-Cat jumps **quickly**.

ADVERBS ANSWER QUESTIONS
Adverbs tell us when, where, how, and how much.

ADVERBS COMPARE VERBS
Adverbs compare actions.

Prepositions
connect nouns and pronouns with other words.

PREPOSITIONAL PHRASE
is a group of words that starts with a preposition.

near the doghouse

Adjectives: Review

Adverbs: Review

Adverbs describe verbs.

Robo-Cat prowls **silently**.
Robo-Snake slithers **sideways**.

ADVERBS ANSWER QUESTIONS
Adverbs tell us when, where, how, and how much.
Adverbs answer questions about verbs.

DID YOU KNOW?
Many adverbs end in -ly

boldly   nervously   colorfully

ADVERBS COMPARE VERBS
Adverbs are words used to compare action verbs.

ONE ACTION
Adverbs describe one action.
Robo-Dog runs **fast**.

TWO ACTIONS
Adverbs compare two actions.
Robo-Dog runs **faster** than Robo-Cat.

THREE OR MORE ACTIONS
Adverbs compare three or more actions.
Of the three pets, Robo-Dog runs the **fastest** of all!

DID YOU KNOW?
Adverbs can also describe adjectives.
Robo-Cat is a **delightfully** quiet pet.

DID YOU KNOW?
Adverbs can also describe other adverbs.
Robo-Dog runs **especially** fast.

Your Turn!
Circle the correct adverb.

Robo-Dog barks **louder / loudest** than Robo-Puppy.

Robo-Cat sleeps **more quietly / most quietly** than Robo-Snake.

Of the three pets, Robo-Cat jumps the **higher / highest**!

Prepositions: Review

Prepositions are connecting words. Prepositions connect nouns and pronouns with other words in a sentence.

PREPOSITIONS SHOW MOVEMENT
along, down, into, toward

Robo-Puppy ran **toward** Robo-Snake.

PREPOSITIONS SHOW WHERE
behind, between, near, over

Robo-Puppy played dead **near** Robo-Snake.

PREPOSITIONS SHOW WHEN
after, before, during, until

Robo-Puppy took a nap **after** lunch.

PREPOSITIONAL PHRASE
A prepositional phrase is a group of words that starts with a preposition.

behind the doghouse
toward the doghouse
beside the doghouse

Robo-Puppy napped **inside the doghouse**.
Where did Robo-Puppy nap?
inside the doghouse

DID YOU KNOW?
A preposition is always the first word in a prepositional phrase.

Your Turn!
Write a preposition in each space. Then circle each prepositional phrase.

Robo-Puppy buried a bone _____ the flowers.

He chewed on Patti's shoe _____ dinner.

Then he hid _____ the doghouse.

Uh-oh, Robo-Puppy! What will Patti say?

Dialogue

*To show that someone is talking in a story, we use **dialogue**.*

"Can you help me?" the old widow asked Detective Davis. "Someone stole my treasure map!"

QUOTATION MARKS
Quotation marks are used when writing dialogue.

"I'll find the thief," said the detective. "Let's look for clues."

DID YOU KNOW?
Quotation marks come in pairs.
One pair always comes at the beginning of the dialogue.
One pair always comes at the end of the dialogue.

"I hid the map in this old vase," insisted Mrs. Williams.
"Now it's gone. We must find it!"
The detective said, "I'd like to talk to the butler."

Your Turn!
Who do you think spoke these dialogues? Choose from the word bank and write a different suspect on each blank line.

cook	butler	parrot	maid

"I didn't do it!"   insisted the _____.

"The parrot stole it,"   accused the _____.

"He's the thief,"   suggested the _____.

"Look upstairs,"   shrieked the _____.

Punctuation

*When writing dialogue, follow the rules for correct **punctuation**.*

PERIODS
In dialogue, a period always goes INSIDE the quotation marks at the end of the quote.

Detective Davis said, "We have four suspects."

COMMAS
In dialogue, a comma always goes INSIDE the quotation marks at the end of the quote.

"I think the parrot is our key suspect," the butler suggested.

EXCLAMATION POINTS AND QUESTION MARKS
These marks go INSIDE or OUTSIDE the quotation marks depending on how they are used.

Put INSIDE the quotes if just the dialogue part is the question or exclamation:

"I agree with the butler!" the maid exclaimed.

Put OUTSIDE the quotes if the whole sentence is a question or exclamation:

Did the parrot say, "I didn't do it"?

Your Turn!
Put a ✓ in the box next to the sentences with correct punctuation.

☐ "Do you really think the parrot took the map"? he asked.

☐ "I think the parrot is guilty," insisted the butler.

☐ The widow said, "It couldn't possibly be the cook".

☐ "Well, it certainly wasn't me!" gasped the maid.

☐ The detective said, "I must look for more clues."

Paragraphs

*Always start a new **paragraph** each time a new person speaks.*

    "I'm not finding any clues," complained the detective. "Are there any more suspects in this house?"
    Mrs. Williams said, "There's only Frank, but he would never steal my treasure map. He doesn't even know I have a treasure map."
    "Who is Frank?" asked the detective.
    "Frank did it!" the parrot squawked.
    "Frank is my grandson," the widow explained.
    "Where is Frank?" Detective Davis asked. "Is he here?"
    "Frank is upstairs in his room," Mrs. Williams said.
    "Frank! Frank!" cried the parrot.

DID YOU KNOW?
Always indent the first line of a new paragraph, even when it starts with dialogue.

Your Turn!

Show where each new paragraph should start by drawing a proofreading symbol to mark each place.

    Frank walked into the room. "Did someone call me?" he asked. "Yes, dear," said Mrs. Williams. "Detective Davis is looking for a thief." "A thief!" exclaimed Frank. "What did the thief steal?" "Someone took your grandmother's treasure map," Detective Davis explained.

Dialogue

To show that someone is talking in a story, we use dialogue.

QUOTATION MARKS
Quotation marks are used when writing dialogue.
"Someone stole my map!" cried Mrs. Williams.

DID YOU KNOW?
Quotation marks come in pairs. One always comes at the beginning of the dialogue. One always comes at the end of the dialogue.

PARAGRAPHS
Always start a new paragraph each time a new person speaks.

PUNCTUATION
When writing dialogue, follow the rules for correct punctuation.

PERIODS OR COMMAS
always go INSIDE the quotation marks at the end of the quote.
Detective Davis said, "We have four suspects."

EXCLAMATION POINTS AND QUESTION MARKS
go INSIDE or OUTSIDE the quotation marks depending on how they are used.

Dialogue Tags

*The **dialogue tag** is the phrase that shows who is speaking.*

"Let's look in the parrot's cage," **suggested Detective Davis.**
"I didn't do it!" **squawked the parrot.**

DID YOU KNOW?
The word said *is the most common word used in a dialogue tag.*

"It's not in the cage," **said** the widow.
She **said**, "Let's look in the kitchen."

DID YOU KNOW?
Here are some words you can use in a dialogue tag.

List 1	List 2	List 3
discuss	groan	yell
shout	cry	whine
thunder	scream	whisper
suggest	observe	sigh
utter	grunt	squeal
mumble	wail	gasp

Your Turn!
Circle the dialogue tags you find in this word search. Use the words from Lists 1 and 2 above. Look forward, backward, up, down, and diagonally.

```
X S C R E A M L A E U Q S O
E H Q R R J D I S C U S S B
L O Z E L M R T Q I R X L S
B U T P P I O K V M G L E E
M T V S Z N A O R G E H S R
U X A I S H R W P Y X J K V
M G T H U N D E R Z R W U E
H K Q W H I N E S W T C O Y
W G R U N T S E G G U S X Z
```

BONUS! Find and circle the words from List 3.

Dialogue Tags

The dialogue tag is the phrase that shows who is speaking.

"I didn't do it!" **cried the parrot.**

DID YOU KNOW?
The word said *is the most common word used in a dialogue tag.*

DID YOU KNOW?
There are many words you can use in a dialogue tag.

agree
bark
beg
comment
cry
declare
discuss
exclaim
gasp
growl
groan
grunt
laugh
mention
mumble
murmur
observe
remark
roar
shout
shriek
sigh
snap
squeal
state
suggest
thunder
urge
utter
wail
whine
whisper
wonder
yell

Position

*The dialogue tag can come in different **positions** in a sentence.*

BEGINNING
Sometimes the dialogue tag is at the beginning of a sentence.

Frank said, "I didn't know Grandmother had a treasure map."

MIDDLE
Sometimes the dialogue tag is in the middle of a sentence.

"She has a treasure map," **Detective Davis explained,** "and she hid it in an old vase."

END
Sometimes the dialogue tag is at the end of a sentence.

"Now the vase is empty," **Mrs. Williams said.**
"Frank did it!" **the parrot squawked.**

Your Turn!
Write the following quote and dialogue tag in three different sentences. In the first sentence, put the dialogue tag in the beginning. In the second sentence, put the dialogue tag in the middle. In the third sentence, put the dialogue tag at the end.

Quote: "Look upstairs and you'll see!"
Dialogue Tag: the parrot squawked

_____
_____
_____
_____
_____
_____
_____
_____

Voice

*You can use dialogue to give each of your characters a strong and unique **voice**.*

Voice: Frank talks like an ordinary boy.

"I found a cool map in that vase," Frank said. "I'm using it to make a craft."

Voice: The parrot talks like a loud bird. He speaks in short sentences and repeats himself.

"Thief! Thief!" accused the parrot.

Voice: Detective Davis talks like he's solving the mystery. He uses words like "clues" and "suspects" when he talks.

"The mystery is solved!" cried Detective Davis. "The parrot's given us clues all along."

Voice: Mrs. Williams talks like a grandmother. She calls Frank "dear."

"Frank, dear, that's the treasure map," the widow explained. "It shows where your grandfather and I buried a treasure chest of gold."

Your Turn!
Write one short sentence of dialogue for each of these characters. Give each of them their own "voice." Have them say what they would do if they found the chest filled with gold.

Frank: _____

_____

Detective Davis: _____

_____

The parrot: _____

_____

Homophones

Homophones are words that **sound** the same but have different meanings and spellings.

LISTEN!
Listen to pairs of homophones.
Hear how they sound the same.

where, wear
Where is the clown's rubber nose? He needs to **wear** it tonight.

LOOK!
Look at the spelling of homophones.
See how they are spelled differently.

meat, meet
Meet the lion tamer. He feeds the lions **meat** for dinner.

LEARN!
Look up unfamiliar homophones in the dictionary.
Learn the different meaning of each word.

"**Morning**" means before noon.
"**Mourning**" means to be sad.

The clowns were **mourning** because their toy car broke that **morning**.

Your Turn!
Circle the homophone that names the picture.

night   knight

bear   bare

knot   not

male   mail

Homophone Word List

Homophones *are words that sound the same but have different meanings and spellings.*

to, two, too
Bonkers the Clown wants **to** eat **two** candy apples **too**.

DID YOU KNOW?
There are many homophone word lists. Try to find different lists online. The list below includes some common homophones.

HOMOPHONE WORD LIST

maid, made
would, wood
bored, board
won, one
ate, eight
buy, by
knows, nose
right, write
they're, their, there

steal, steel
tow, toe
sum, some
site, sight, cite
cell, sell
flower, flour
piece, peace
stare, stair
week, weak

Your Turn!
Help Bonkers drive in and out of the maze, collecting as many homophones as he can. Be careful! Bonkers must pass through the center of the maze on his way back to the exit. Don't cross over his path or go through the same opening twice.

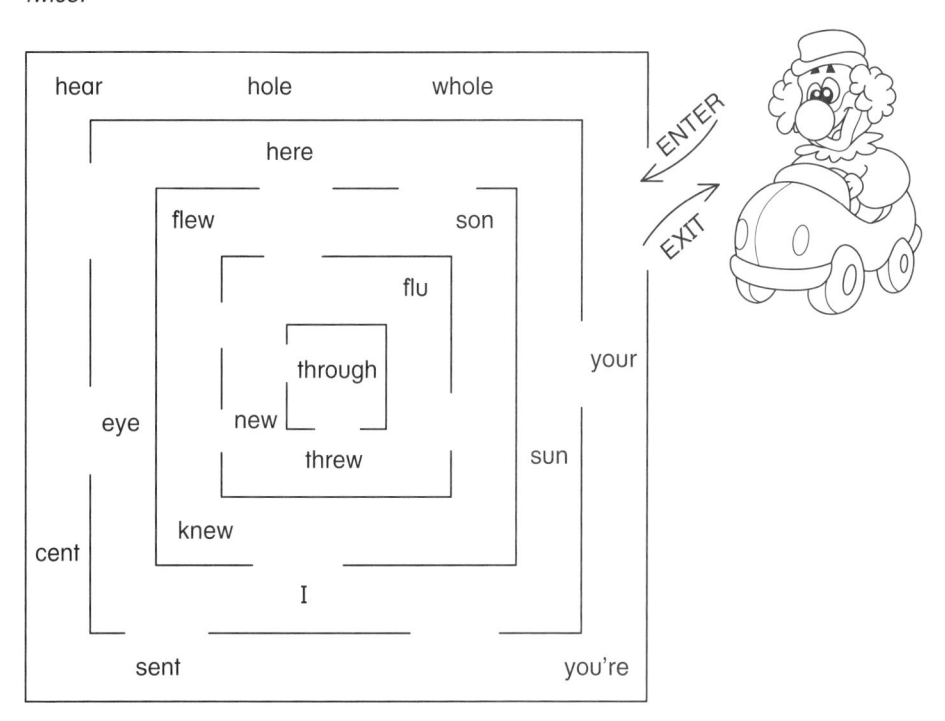

Maze words:
hear, hole, whole
here
flew, son
flu
through
eye, new, your
threw, sun
cent, knew
I
sent, you're

ENTER / EXIT

Homographs

Homographs are words that are **spelled** the same but sound different and have different meanings.

The clown tied the lion's tail in a **bow**.

The elephant took a **bow** after the performance.

Your Turn!
Write the homographs from the word bank on the correct blanks in these sentences.

Word bank: does   bass   dove   wound

The ringmaster _____ a rope around the pole.

The acrobat _____ amazing tricks on the high wire!

The clown jumped and _____ into a bucket of water.

One clown played the _____ guitar.

Look at the two fawns and three _____ in the pen.

See the trained _____ fly through the hoop!

One of the lions has a _____ on its paw.

The clown fished in a pond and caught a giant _____.

Homophones are words that sound the same but have different meanings and spellings.

LISTEN!
Listen how they sound the same.

where, wear

LOOK!
See how they are spelled differently.

meat, meet

LEARN!
Learn the different meaning of each word.

morning, mourning

WORD LIST
to, two, too
would, wood
bored, board
won, one
ate, eight
bear, bare
know, no
knows, nose
right, write
they're, their, there
steal, steel
tow, toe
sum, some
site, sight, cite
cell, sell
flower, flour
him, hymn
piece, peace
stare, stair
week, weak

Homographs
are words that are spelled the same but sound different and have different meanings.

The clown tied the lion's tail in a **bow**.

The elephant took a **bow** after the performance.

Homonyms
Some homonyms are spelled the same and sound the same but have different meanings.

There is a **fly** buzzing near the lion's cage.

The acrobats will **fly** through the air on a trapeze.

DID YOU KNOW?
Homonyms, homophones, and homographs can be confusing.

It's easy to make a spelling mistake.

Use a dictionary to help.

Homonyms

*Some **homonyms** are spelled the same and sound the same but have different meanings.*

There is a **fly** buzzing near the lion's cage.
The acrobats will **fly** through the air.

DID YOU KNOW?
Other words in the sentence give clues to help understand the meaning of the homonym.

The clown popped the balloon with a **pin**.
The clown will **pin** a flower on his collar.

DID YOU KNOW?
Homonyms can also include homophones and homographs.

Homonyms, homophones, and homographs can be confusing. It's easy to make a spelling mistake. Use a dictionary to help.

Your Turn!
Use the Secret Code to decode and spell the two homonyms below. Then write a sentence using any pair of homonyms.

Secret Code:

A	B	C	D	E	F	G	H	I	J	K	L	M
Z	Y	X	W	V	U	T	S	R	Q	P	O	N

N	O	P	Q	R	S	T	U	V	W	X	Y	Z
M	L	K	J	I	H	G	F	E	D	C	B	A

__ __ __ __ __
W Z M X V

__ __ __
K V G

_____
_____
_____
_____

Homonyms

Homonym Word List

*Some **homonyms** are words that are spelled the same and sound the same but have different meanings. Many homonyms have one meaning when used as a noun and a different meaning when used as a verb.*

HOMONYM WORD LIST

ring: Dancing dogs **ring** bells as they prance around the **ring**.

report: A clown **reports** the news in his silly **report**.

whistle: The lion tamer **whistled** to the lions on his **whistle**.

row: Children sat in a **row** to watch the clowns **row** a boat.

spy: A **spy** will **spy** on the clown.

oil: **Oil** the clown's rusty car with a special **oil**.

shovel: **Shovel** the oats with the wide **shovel**.

brush: Use the blue **brush** to **brush** the horse's mane.

paint: Did Bonkers **paint** the circus tent with red **paint**?

Your Turn!

Write two sentences for each homonym. In one sentence, write the homonym as a verb. In the other sentence, write the homonym as a noun.

park

Verb: _____

_____

Noun: _____

_____

roll

Verb: _____

_____

Noun: _____

_____

Fun with Words

*Homophones, homographs, and homonyms are **fun to use**!*

JOKES
Use them to write jokes, riddles, and cartoons.

Why did the cat jump down out of the tree?
Because it saw the tree **bark**.

Why did the queen draw straight lines?
Because she was the **ruler**.

What is the tallest building in the world?
The library. It has the most **stories**.

POETRY
Use them to write poetry.

Rhyming Poems:

The Last Pear

I choose the last delicious **pear**,
And wish I had another **pair**.
I bite it and a crunch I **hear**,
Aren't there any more in **here**?

Haiku:
Brown **fur** in the snow
Sleeping under the **fir** tree
Hibernating cub

Your Turn!
Underline the correct words in each joke.

Q: Why do bumblebees hum?

A: They don't **no / know** the words.

Q: Why is the bread full of **wholes / holes**?

A: Because it's **whole / hole** wheat bread.

Five Paragraphs

You can write a story or a report using **five paragraphs**.

DID YOU KNOW?
Each paragraph does an important job.

FORMAT
Introduction: Paragraph #1
   This paragraph introduces the story or report.

Body: Paragraphs #2, #3, #4
   These 3 paragraphs tell 3 subtopics or ideas about the main topic.

Closing: Paragraph #5
   This paragraph brings the story or report to an end.

DID YOU KNOW?
You can have <u>more</u> than three paragraphs in the **BODY**, but three is a good number.

Your Turn!
Underline three subtopics you might choose to write about for each main topic.

Main Topic:	Subtopics:
dinosaurs:	T. rex, Triceratops, extinct, predators, eggs and young, giant lizards
space:	constellations, the sun, black holes, comets, gravity, astronomy, telescope
astronauts:	rocket ship, space suit, women in space, Neil Armstrong, NASA, gear
weather:	temperature, rain and snow, air pressure, winds, weather instruments, humidity
my day at the zoo:	zebras, giraffes, meerkats, polar bears, lions, reptile house, tram ride

Kinds of Writing

When writing a five-paragraph story or report, you will use one of three kinds of writing. Here are some examples.

NARRATIVE
Narrative writing tells a story.
   Fiction: Tell a make-believe story.
   Nonfiction: Tell a story about something true.

EXPOSITORY
Expository writing explains.
   Explain step-by-step how to make cookies.
   Explain how a dump truck works.
   Explain why bees like flowers.

PERSUASIVE
Persuasive writing persuades or convinces.
   Persuade your brother to buy a game.
   Persuade your friend to be honest.
   Persuade your town to build a park.

Your Turn!
*Which kind of writing would you use to do the following? Write the word **narrative**, **expository**, or **persuasive** on each blank line.*

1. Explain how to make a toy rocket ship.
   _____

2. Tell a story about your last birthday.
   _____

3. Convince your grandma to get a goldfish.
   _____

4. Tell an imaginary story about living in a castle.
   _____

5. Persuade your friend to go camping with you.
   _____

6. Explain why birds build nests.
   _____

Transitions

*The words or phrases we use to move from one paragraph to the next are called **transitions**. Transitions help readers connect the ideas in a story. They help stories flow together smoothly.*

EXAMPLE
The word "first" is the transition between the first paragraph and the second paragraph.

The Best Day

When I won the raffle, I got to spend a day with my favorite baseball team, the Angels. I ate breakfast with the team. I stood next to the shortstop during practice. I even got to be a batboy during the game. It was my best day ever!

First, I ate breakfast with all the players at the stadium…

DID YOU KNOW?
"Transition" means to move from one to another.

DID YOU KNOW?
There are many words you can use for transitions. Here are just a few.

LIST OF TRANSITIONS

First	Next	Later
Then	Also	Along with
Another	After	Last of all
Finally	At dawn	

Your Turn!
Find and circle the transitions from the list. Words are hidden in every direction!

```
P X B Q G Z C W L A
A L A S T O F A L L
T R F I R S T X Y O
D E Z K Q E H L Q N
A H W X R J L Z B G
W T O S L A M F C W
N O D B N E X T W I
V N Q I Z S N E H T
R A F T E R W F X H
```

Five Paragraphs

You can write a story or a report using five paragraphs.

DID YOU KNOW?
Each paragraph has an important job to do.

FORMAT

Introduction: Paragraph #1 introduces the story or report.

Body: Paragraphs #2, #3, and #4 tell three ideas about the main topic.

Closing: Paragraph #5 brings the story or report to an end.

Three Kinds of Writing

NARRATIVE
Tells a story that can be:
- make-believe
- true

EXPOSITORY
Explains:
- how to make something
- how something works
- why something happens

PERSUASIVE
Persuades someone:
- to buy something
- to do something
- to like something

TRANSITIONS
First
Second
Next
Then
Also
After
After that
Along with
Another
Later
Last of all
Finally

Introduction

*The first paragraph **introduces** the story or report.*

The Best Day

When I won the raffle, I got to spend a day with my favorite baseball team, the Angels. I ate breakfast with the team. I stood next to the shortstop during practice. I even got to be a batboy during the game. It was my best day ever!

    First, I ate breakfast with all the players at the stadium…

DID YOU KNOW?
*Each sentence in the **introduction** has an important job to do.*

Sentence #1 introduces the main idea of the story or report.

Sentence #2 tells about the first subtopic or idea you'll write about in Paragraph #2.

Sentence #3 tells about the second subtopic or idea you'll write about in Paragraph #3.

Sentence #4 tells about the third subtopic or idea you'll write about in Paragraph #4.

Sentence #5 wraps up the paragraph or transitions into the next paragraph.

DID YOU KNOW?
You can have more than three sentences in the middle of the paragraph, but three is a good number.

Your Turn!
Read "The Best Day" (above). Then write one word that tells the subtopic or idea for each of these sentences in the story.

#2: I ate _____.

#3: During practice, I stood next to the _____.

#4: At the game, I was _____.

Body

*The three paragraphs in the middle of the story or report are called the **body**. These three paragraphs tell three subtopics or ideas about the main topic.*

PARAGRAPH #2
    First, I ate breakfast with all the players at the stadium. Don Garcia, the pitcher, sat next to me. We had blueberry pancakes. Don Garcia signed a baseball and gave it to me. I couldn't believe this special day was happening!

PARAGRAPH #3
    After breakfast was finished, I went with the team to the field for practice. The manager told me to stand next to the shortstop. It felt scary and fun to be standing in the middle of that big field with all the action happening around me. Once, the ball landed at my feet so I picked it up and threw it to Don Garcia. All the players were really nice.

PARAGRAPH #4
    At 3:00, the big game started. I was batboy during the game. If a player's bat broke, I ran out and gave him a new one. Then I picked up the broken pieces. When the umpire needed a new ball, I ran out and handed it to him. It was hard work!

DID YOU KNOW?
*In every paragraph of the **body**, each sentence has an important job to do.*

Sentence #1 introduces the subtopic. It often has a transition word in it.
Sentence #2 tells one detail about the subtopic.
Sentence #3 tells a second detail.
Sentence #4 tells a third detail.
Sentence #5 wraps up the paragraph or transitions into the next paragraph.

Your Turn!
Underline the sentence in each paragraph that introduces Paragraphs #2, #3, and #4 above.

Closing

*This paragraph brings the story or report to an **end**.*

DID YOU KNOW?
Paragraph #5 can be as long or as short as you want. It just needs to wrap up the story or report in a satisfying way.

The Best Day

    When I won the raffle, I got to spend a day with my favorite baseball team, the Angels. I ate breakfast with the team. I stood next to the shortstop during practice. I even got to be a batboy during the game. It was my best day ever!

    First, I ate breakfast with all the players at the stadium. Don Garcia, the pitcher, sat next to me. We had blueberry pancakes. The pitcher signed a baseball and gave it to me. I couldn't believe this special day was happening!

    After breakfast was finished, I went with the team to the field for practice. The manager told me to stand next to the shortstop. It felt scary and fun to be standing in the middle of that big field with all the action happening around me. Once, the ball landed at my feet so I picked it up and threw it to Don Garcia. All the players were really nice.

    At 3:00, the big game started. I was batboy during the game. If a player's bat broke, I ran out and gave him a new one. Then I picked up the broken pieces. When the umpire needed a new ball, I ran out and handed it to him. It was hard work!

    When Dad picked me up after the game, I was tired. But I felt more excited than I had ever felt in my life. I still couldn't believe I won the raffle to spend a day with the Angels. My ticket had the winning number, and it was a winning day!

Your Turn!
Circle the closing in the example above.
Clue: You will circle an entire paragraph.

Prefix List

*A prefix is added to the beginning of a word to make a new word. Here is a list of common **prefixes**, their meanings, and the words they are used in.*

Learning the meaning of a prefix can help you understand the meaning of new words.

PREFIX	MEANING	WORDS
anti-	opposite	antifreeze, antibacterial
audi-	to hear	audience, auditorium, audiobook
auto-	self	autobiography, automobile
biblio-	book	bibliography
bio-	life	biology, biodegradable
circum-	around	circumference, circumstance
co-	together	cooperate, coordinate, copilot
de-	opposite	deforest, dehydrate
demo-	people	democracy, democrat
eco-	environment	ecology, ecosystem
ex-	out	exit, exclude, exoskeleton
micro-	small	microscope, microorganism
milli-	thousandth	millimeter, milligram
multi-	many	multicultural, multimillionaire
pre-	before	prefix, precaution, preview
re-	again	reflection, repair, reopen
sub-	below	subway, submarine, subheading
tele-	far	telescope, television, telephone
trans-	across	transport, transfusion, transatlantic
un-	not	unhappy, unripe, unknown, unfriendly

Your Turn!

Underline the prefix in each word. Then look up these words in the dictionary. Write their definitions on the blank lines.

autobiography: _____

circumference: _____

dehydrate: _____

telescope: _____

Lesson 8 Prefixes and Suffixes | PAGE 1

Root Words

Some words are made up of different parts.
*The main part of the word is called the **root word**.*

Unicycle
The root word is "cycle," which means wheel.
The prefix is "uni," which means one.
uni + cycle = having one wheel

DID YOU KNOW?
A root word is also called a base word.

> A prefix is attached to the beginning of a root word to change its meaning.

prefix + root word = new word
uni + cycle = unicycle, having one wheel
bi + cycle = bicycle, having two wheels
tri + cycle = tricycle, having three wheels

DID YOU KNOW?
Changing the prefix changes the meaning of the word.

Your Turn!
*Look up the root word **-corn** in the dictionary. Answer the question, then circle the root word in each word below.*

What is the meaning of the root word **-corn**?

_____

Draw a picture of Uni the Unicorn with one horn, with two horns, and with three horns.

unicorn	bicorn	tricorn

Lesson 8 Prefixes and Suffixes | PAGE 3

Numerical Prefixes

Some prefixes mean different numbers.

PREFIX	MEANING	WORDS
uni-	1	unicorn, unicycle
bi-	2	bicycle, bicentennial
tri-	3	tricycle, trilogy
quad-	4	quadrilateral, quadruplets
penta-	5	pentagon, pentathlon
octo-	8	octopus, octagon
deca-	10	decade, decapod
centi-	100	centipede, centimeter

Your Turn!
Draw these different shapes.

pentagon

quadrilateral

octagon

Numerical Prefixes

Prefix

*A prefix is added to the **beginning** of a word.*

PREFIX	MEANING
anti-	opposite
audi-	to hear
auto-	self
biblio-	books
bio-	life
circum-	around
co-	together
de-	opposite
demo-	people
eco-	environment

ROOT WORDS
*The main part of the word is the **root word**.*

NUMERICAL PREFIXES
Some prefixes mean different numbers.

uni-   = 1
bi-   = 2
tri-   = 3
quad-   = 4
penta- = 5
octo-   = 8
deca-   = 10
centi- = 100

bi-   bifocals
tri-   tricycle
octo- octopus

Suffix

*A suffix is added to the **end** of a word.*

A suffix changes how the word is used.

Root Word: bright

bright + en = brighten (verb)

bright + ly = brightly (adverb)

bright + er = brighter (adjective)

bright + ness = brightness (noun)

SUFFIX	MEANING
-able	capable of
-ation	that which is
-ed	past
-er	one who
-en	made of
-est	most
-fy	to make
-ing	action of
-less	without
-ment	act of doing
-ology	study of
-ship	quality of
-y	characterized by

PREFIXES AND SUFFIXES

Some root words have both a prefix and a suffix.

disagreement
transportation

Suffixes

*A **suffix** is added to the end of a word to make a new word.*

Changing the suffix changes the way a word is used in a sentence.

Root word: bright
bright + **en** = brighten **(verb)**
bright + **ly** = brightly **(adverb)**
bright + **er** = brighter **(adjective)**
bright + **ness** = brightness **(noun)**

Your Turn!
Add a suffix to each of these words to make a new word.

Root word: *soft*
Noun: soft + _____ = _____
Verb: soft + _____ = _____

Root word: *loud*
Adverb: loud + _____ = _____
Noun: loud + _____ = _____

Root word: *tight*
Adjective: tight + _____ = _____
Verb: tight + _____ = _____

Root word: *quiet*
Adverb: quiet + _____ = _____
Adjective: quiet + _____ = _____

Suffixes

Prefixes and Suffixes

*Some root words have both a **prefix** and a **suffix**.*

depend
depend + ence = dependence
in + depend + ence = independence

agree
agree + ment = agreement
dis + agree + ment = disagreement

port
trans + port = transport
trans + port + ation = transportation

honor
dis + honor = dishonor
dis + honor + able = dishonorable

kind
kind + ness = kindness
un + kind + ness = unkindness

Look up words in the dictionary to check their spelling and their meaning.

Your Turn!
Draw a line from each word to its definition.

dependence	the act of carrying
independence	something mean or cruel
transport	being influenced by something or someone
transportation	a nice thing
kindness	to take from one place to another
unkindness	freedom from another

Suffix List

*Here is a list of common **suffixes**, their meanings, and the words they are used in.*

Learning the meaning of a suffix can help you understand the meaning of new words.

SUFFIX	MEANING	WORDS
-able	capable of	comfortable, honorable
-ation	that which is	complication, irritation
-ed	past	yelled, climbed, hunted
-er	one who	worker, runner, teacher
-en	made of	wooden, woolen, rotten
-ence	state or condition	absence, obedience
-est	most	fastest, longest
-fy	make	beautify, magnify
-ing	action of	barking, smelling
-ish	like	childish, foolish
-ist	person who does	artist, biologist, dentist
-less	without	homeless, hopeless
-let	small	inlet, piglet
-ment	act of doing	movement, excitement
-ness	state of being	blindness, quietness
-ology	study of	geology, biology, mythology
-ship	quality of	friendship, leadership
-tion	act of or state of	reaction, election, motion
-y	characterized by	watery, sleepy, frosty

Your Turn!

Underline the suffix in each word. Then look up these words in the dictionary. Write their definitions on the blank lines.

inlet: _____

magnify: _____

biology: _____

woolen: _____

Compound Words

*When two or more words are joined together to make a new word, the new word is called a **compound word**.*

some + thing = something
flower + pot = flowerpot

Nora planted something in her **flowerpot**.

door + bell = doorbell

Nora heard the **doorbell** ring.
She answered the door.
It was her friend, Lucas.

DID YOU KNOW?
There are 3 kinds of compound words:

Closed: One or more words form one whole new word.

  football

Hyphenated: One or more words form a new word using hyphens.

  merry-go-round

Open: Two separate words form one new meaning, but the words are not joined together.

  ice skates

Your Turn!
Draw a line joining one word on the left with one word on the right to make a closed compound word.

cup   keeper
hair   town
air   book
zoo   plane
pop   brush
down   cake
note   corn

Lesson 9 Compound Words | PAGE 2

Hyphenated Compounds

*When words are joined together with hyphens to form a compound word, it is the **hyphenated** form.*

editor-in-chief
sister-in-law
runner-up
merry-go-round
jack-in-the-box

Nora is the **editor-in-chief** of a science magazine for kids. She loves doing strange experiments!

DID YOU KNOW?
You can use a dictionary to check the spelling of a compound word.

Your Turn!
Unscramble these compound words. Write their correct spelling on the blank lines. Then answer the riddle below.

ons-ni-awl: __ __ __ - __ __ - __ __ __
                                       1

wonk-ti-lal: __ __ __ __ - __ __ - __ __ __
                     4

arey-den: __ __ __ __ - __ __ __
                  2

slef-etidnig:
__ __ __ __ - __ __ __ __ __
                              5

net-raye-lod:
__ __ __ - __ __ __ __ - __ __ __
              3

Riddle: *Which word is spelled wrong in the dictionary?*

__ __ __ __ __
 1 2 3 4 5

Hyphenated Compounds

Open Compounds

*When two separate words form one new meaning but the words are not joined together, it is the **open** form of a compound word.*

full + moon = full moon
   Last night there was a **full moon**.

post + office = post office
   Nora got a strange box from the **post office**.

best + friend + forever = best friend forever
   It was from Beckie, Nora's **best friend forever**. Inside the box was a seed. Nora planted the seed, and a tree grew in just one day!

ice + cream = ice cream
   It was a tree with fruit like **ice cream**.

Your Turn!
Place these compound words into the word puzzle where they fit best.

CELL PHONE
FRENCH FRY
NEW WORLD
FINE ART
HOT DOG

Compound Words

When two or more words are joined together to make a new word, the new word is called a compound word.

DID YOU KNOW?
There are 3 kinds of compound words.

Closed:
forms one whole new word
football

Hyphenated:
forms a new word using hyphens
merry-go-round

Open:
two separate words form one new meaning, but the words are not joined together
ice skates

DID YOU KNOW?
You can use a dictionary to check the spelling of a compound word.

Compound Numbers

When you spell out compound numbers from 21 to 99, write them using hyphens.

twenty + five = twenty-five
thirty + eight = thirty-eight
ninety + nine = ninety-nine

"I am doing an experiment," Nora told Lucas. "I invented a special formula to grow money."

"How does it work?" Lucas asked. "Yesterday I planted a quarter that I painted with my formula," Nora said. "Today a plant grew with **twenty-five** quarters on it."

"Last week I planted a nickel," she explained. "A plant grew with **thirty-eight** nickels on it."

Nora showed Lucas her flowerpot. "I just planted a penny. I hope a plant grows with **ninety-nine** pennies on it!"

DID YOU KNOW?
Fractions are also spelled out as compound numbers.

two-thirds
one-fourth
three-fifths

Your Turn!
Write the correct spelling of these compound numbers and fractions:

51: _____
67: _____
1/2: _____
22: _____

Compound Numbers

When you spell out compound numbers from 21 to 99, write them using hyphens.

twenty + five = twenty-five

thirty + eight = thirty-eight

Compound Plurals

Compound words form plurals in different ways.

Closed form: The closed form of compound words follow the standard rules for forming plural nouns.

blackberry = blackberries

Hyphenated form: The strongest or most important word is made plural.

runner-up = runners-up

Open form: The strongest or most important word is made plural.

major general = majors general

paper clip = paper clips

Compound Plurals

*Compound words form **plurals** in different ways.*

CLOSED FORM:
The closed form of compound words follows the standard rules for forming plural nouns.

blackberry = blackberries
   Nora did a new experiment with a **blackberry** bush.
   It grew **blackberries** that looked like real dimes.

HYPHENATED FORM:
The strongest or most important word is made plural, even if it is in the middle.

runner-up = runners-up
   Nora was the **runner-up** in the Science Fair.
   Nora and Beckie were the **runners-up** in the Science Fair.

OPEN FORM:
The strongest or most important word in the compound word is made plural.

major general = **majors** general

paper clip = paper **clips**

Your Turn!
Write the plurals of each compound word on these blank lines.

mother-in-law: _____

post office: _____

fingernail: _____

toothbrush: _____

editor-in-chief: _____

Compound Adjectives

*When compound words are used as **adjectives**, they take different forms depending on where they are positioned in the sentence.*

Before the noun:
If the adjective comes **before** the noun, it **uses** hyphens.
Nora's **zebra-striped** tree was famous.
(The noun is *tree*.)

After the noun:
If the adjective comes **after** the noun, it **does not use** hyphens.
Nora's tree was **zebra striped**.
(The noun is *tree*.)

Before the noun:
Her **get-rich-quick** plan worked.
(The noun is *plan*.)

After the noun:
Her plan to **get rich quick** worked.
(The noun is *plan*.)

DID YOU KNOW?
Here's how to figure out when to use hyphens in a compound adjective.
First, find the noun. Then find the adjective that describes it.
If the compound adjective comes <u>before</u> the noun, use a hyphen.

Your Turn!
Circle the correct form of the adjective in each sentence.

Oh no! Nora's **well-mannered / well mannered** dog, Sparkplug, dug up all her plants!

Sparkplug was not **well-mannered / well mannered** after all!

Now Nora will start **brand-new / brand new** experiments.

Her experiments will be **brand-new / brand new**.

Strong Words

*Some words are common or overused. We call these weak words. Try to replace weak words with **strong and interesting words**.*

HERE'S WHAT TO DO:
1. Write down a weak word.
2. Look up that word in a thesaurus.
3. Write down a list of synonyms for that word.
4. Choose a **synonym** to write a **strong word** instead.

EXAMPLE
The turtles **eat** flies and crickets.

Weak Word: eat
Synonyms: swallow, gobble, gulp

The turtles **swallow** flies and crickets.
The turtles **gobble** up flies and crickets.
The turtles **gulp** down flies and crickets.

Your Turn!
Draw a line from each weak word to its synonym.

Weak Word	Strong Word
walk	slurp
drink	doze
look	squat
sleep	stroll
sit	peek

Lesson 10 Synonyms and Antonyms | PAGE 2

Strong Paragraphs

*Don't repeat the same word twice in the same paragraph. That is weak writing. Instead, use synonyms to write **strong paragraphs**.*

DID YOU KNOW?
It is okay to repeat some words in the same paragraph. Most of the time, though, try not to repeat a main word.

HERE'S WHAT TO DO:
1. Read a paragraph that you wrote.
2. Circle words you repeat in the same paragraph.
3. Look them up in a thesaurus, or think of other words you know.
4. Choose **synonyms** to write **different words** instead.

EXAMPLE:
   The boa constrictor sleeps in his cage. This boa constrictor likes to sleep under the heat lamp. I want to get a boa constrictor like the one I saw sleeping in his cage at the Reptile Zoo.

REPEATED WORDS	SYNONYMS
boa constrictor	snake, reptile
sleep	nap, doze
cage	terrarium, box

Your Turn!
Replace repeated words with synonyms.

   The boa constrictor sleeps in his cage. This

_____ likes to _____ under the heat lamp. I
(boa constrictor)   (sleep)

want to get a _____ like the one I saw _____
                 (boa constrictor)   (sleeping)

in his _____ at the Reptile Zoo.
         (cage)

Strong Paragraphs

Synonyms

*Words that mean the same are called **synonyms**.*

WORD   **SYNONYMS**
lizard   gecko, chameleon
cage   terrarium, pen, box
walk   creep, stroll, scurry
big   enormous, huge, gigantic
nice   attractive, pleasant, polite

DID YOU KNOW?
You can find synonyms for most words in a thesaurus.

Your Turn!
*Look up each word in a thesaurus. Write two or more **synonyms** for each word on the blank lines.*

climb: _____

_____

little: _____

_____

hide: _____

_____

Synonyms
Words that mean the same are called synonyms.

cage
terrarium
pen

walk
squat
scurry

big
huge
gigantic

STRONG WORDS
Weak words are those that are overused.

*Choose a **synonym** to write a **strong word** instead.*

STRONG PARAGRAPHS
Don't repeat the same main word twice in the same paragraph.

*Choose **synonyms** to write **different words** instead.*

Antonyms
Words that mean the opposite are called antonyms.

inside/outside
long/short
rough/smooth
adult/baby

HUMOR
Use antonyms to add humor!

The turtles **climbed up**.
Crash! Splash!
The turtles **fell down**.

CHARACTERS
Try using antonyms! Opposites make interesting characters.

Gabi is **big**.
Lex is **little**.

Gabi is **aggressive**.
Lex is **shy**.

Gabi likes **loud** music.
Lex likes **quiet** music.

DID YOU KNOW?
You can have one character with two opposite traits.

OR...

You can have two characters that are opposite.

Antonyms

*Words that mean the opposite are called **antonyms**.*

fast iguana
slow tortoise

thin garter snake
plump boa constrictor

WORD	ANTONYM
inside	outside
long	short
rough	smooth
adult	baby
ugly	pretty

DID YOU KNOW?
You can find antonyms for many words in a thesaurus.

Your Turn!
*Look up each word in a thesaurus. Write one or more **antonyms** for each word on the blank lines.*

often: _____
_____

happy: _____
_____

safety: _____
_____

Humor

*If you want to add **humor** to a story, try using antonyms!*

The turtles **climbed up** on each other in a tall stack.
The biggest turtle perched on top.
Flies buzzed quickly around their heads.
The smallest turtle reached out slowly to catch a fly.
Crash! Splash! The turtles **fell down** in a pile.

WORD	ANTONYM
climbed	fell
up	down
biggest	smallest
quickly	slowly

DID YOU KNOW?
Opposites often make people laugh.

Your Turn!
Unscramble each antonym and write it on the blank line.

Word	Antonym
wet	ryd: _____
tall	thors: _____
lumpy	hotoms: _____

Humor

Characters

*When developing **characters** in your story, try using antonyms! Opposites make interesting characters.*

Gabi Gila Monster drinks **cold** soda pop.
Lex Gecko drinks **hot** cocoa.

Gabi lives **up north**. Lex lives **down south**.

Gabi is **big**. Lex is **little**.

Gabi is **aggressive**. Lex is **shy**.

Gabi likes **loud** music. Lex likes **quiet** music.

Together, they are the Leapin' Lizard Detectives!

DID YOU KNOW?
You can have one character with two opposite traits.

OR...

You can have two characters who are opposite.

Your Turn!
Write antonyms that tell us more about Gabi and Lex. Look up words in a thesaurus for ideas.

Gabi types text messages **quickly**.

Lex types _____.

Gabi wakes up **early**.

Lex wakes up _____.

Gabi likes **sweet** strawberries.

Lex likes _____ lemons.

Gabi likes _____ weather.

Lex likes _____ weather.

Answer Key

Level 2 Fold-N-Go® Grammar Pack
Remove Answer Key and store in a notebook or folder.

Lesson 1 - Sentences

Page 1: Simple Subject
knight, He, They, princess, She

Page 2: Complete Subject
(The lovely princess) aimed at the moat.
(Her sharp arrow) got stuck in a tree trunk!
(The sleek horse) trotted over to the oak tree.
(The strong, muscular knight) pulled out the arrow.

Page 3: Simple Predicate
drew, shut, flapped, was, came

Page 4: Complete Predicate
Answers will vary.

Page 5: Compound Subject
The <u>knight</u> and the <u>princess</u>

Page 6: Compound Predicate
shot, hit, won
trotted, galloped, raced
clapped, cheered

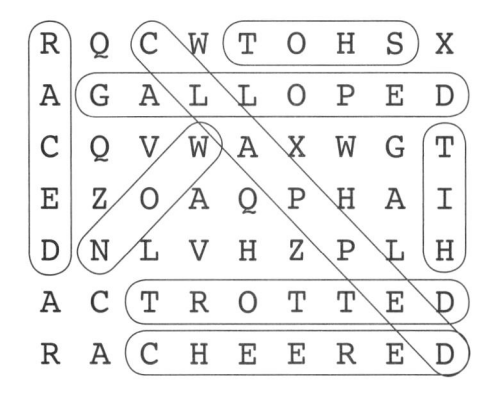

Lesson 2 – Four Sentences

Page 1: Declarative Sentence
Tori picked up the phone.
She called her friend, Levi.
Tori asked Levi to go to Adventure Park.

Page 2: Interrogative Sentence
<u>What does Levi like to do the most at Adventure Park?</u>
He likes to play in the slimy mud pit.
<u>What is Tori's favorite thing to do at Adventure Park?</u>
She likes to get a hammer and nails and build a fort.
<u>Which one would you like to do the most?</u>

Page 3: Imperative Sentence
Suggested answers:

Please wash the mud off your feet. (Or, Wash the mud off your feet, please.)
Pound the nail harder.
Bring Tori a water bottle.

Page 4: Exclamatory Sentence
Tori and Levi wanted to play in the mud all day!
They had never been so muddy!
Levi built the tallest fort ever!
They had tons of fun!

Page 5: Sentence Fragments
Cryptogram solution (secret message): **EVERY SENTENCE HAS A SUBJECT AND A PREDICATE.**

Solution Tip: *Explain that this is a deductive reasoning puzzle, and using logic will help students arrive at a conclusion. For example, notice that two words have just one letter, and both have a Q beneath them. There are only two one-letter words in English: I and a. It's more likely that the blanks represent the letter a, so students can plug A into five blank spots.*

The last word ends in the code letters TQPJ. You know that T=C, Q=A, P=T, and J=E. So the word ends in -CATE (predicate). Now that there are many more letters solved, plug those into the other spots. From this point, it should be easy to figure out the rest of the puzzle.

Page 6: Run-on Sentences
Answers will vary. Possible answers include:

On the way home, Tori asked Levi what he liked most about Adventure Park. ~~and~~ He said he used to like the mud pit the best, but not anymore. ~~because~~ He had so much fun building the fort with Tori that now he liked that part the best. ~~and~~ Then Levi asked Tori about her favorite part.

Lesson 3 – Compound Sentences

Page 1: Compound Sentences
<u>One day Emma's family went camping</u>, and <u>her cousin Nick came with them</u>.
<u>Ollie wanted to go along</u>, so <u>they brought him, too</u>.
<u>They saw caribou</u>, but <u>the caribou galloped away</u>.
<u>Soon they found a place to camp</u>, and <u>they put up their tent</u>.
<u>The cousins felt safe</u>, for <u>they didn't see any polar bears</u>.

Page 2: Two Sentences
Answers will vary.

Fragments are:
Emma's parka and boots,
(and) an igloo and sleds.

Page 3: Conjunctions

```
X  O  R  G  J  S  D  L
C  V  M  W  Q  O  B  A
K  H  P  F  Z  M  Y  N
T  S  L  V  R  O  F  D
U  Y  W  X  R  J  H  M
B  M  G  O  K  P  L  C
Q  X  N  N  T  E  Y  Z
```

Page 4: Commas
Nick helped Emma get in her kayak**,** and they both went back to shore.
The seal followed them**,** but Ollie started to bark.
The seal tossed a ball of moss to Ollie**,** so Ollie played fetch.
Emma gave the seal a snack**,** for it looked hungry.

Page 5: Choosing Conjunctions
Answers will vary.

Page 6: Sentence Length
Answers will vary. Here are several ways to create one compound sentence from two short sentences:

It was held every summer, and all the villagers gathered.
All the villagers gathered, and everyone held tightly to a walrus skin.
Emma was invited to go first, so she stood on the walrus skin.
Then she bounced, for it was like being on a trampoline.

Lesson 4 - Parts of Speech Answer Key

Page 1: Nouns: Review

Answers will vary. Make sure answers include both common and proper nouns.

Page 2: Verbs: Review

Robo-Dog (walked) with Patti to the store.
He (will perform) tricks for her friends.
He (is) the happiest robot dog in the world!

Page 3: Pronouns: Review

me   her
they   you
she   mine

Page 4: Adjectives: Review

stronger
friendlier
scariest

Page 5: Adverbs: Review

louder
more quietly
highest

Page 6: Prepositions: Review

Answers will vary.

Robo-Puppy buried a bone _____ the flowers.
Possible answers: under, beneath, between, near, next to

He chewed on Patti's shoe _____ dinner.
Possible answers: before, after, during

Then he hid _____ the doghouse.
Possible answers: beside, behind, inside, near

Lesson 5 - Dialogue

Page 1: Dialogue
Answers will vary.

Page 2: Punctuation
☐ "Do you really think the parrot took the map"? he asked.
☑ "I think the parrot is guilty," insisted the butler.
☐ The widow said, "It couldn't possibly be the cook".
☑ "Well, it certainly wasn't me!" gasped the maid.
☑ The detective said, "I must look for more clues. "

Page 3: Paragraphs

    Frank walked into the room. "Did someone call me?" he asked. ¶ "Yes, dear," said Mrs. Williams. "Detective Davis is looking for a thief." ¶ "A thief!" exclaimed Frank. "What did the thief steal?" ¶ "Someone took your grandmother's treasure map," Detective Davis explained.

Page 4: Dialogue Tags

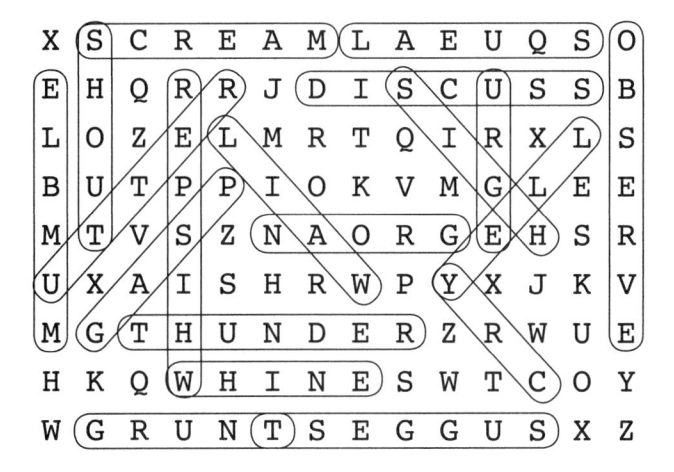

```
X  S  C  R  E  A  M  L  A  E  U  Q  S  O
E  H  Q  R  R  J  D  I  S  C  U  S  S  B
L  O  Z  E  L  M  R  T  Q  I  R  X  L  S
B  U  T  P  P  I  O  K  V  M  G  L  E  E
M  T  V  S  Z  N  A  O  R  G  E  H  S  R
U  X  A  I  S  H  R  W  P  Y  X  J  K  V
M  G  T  H  U  N  D  E  R  Z  R  W  U  E
H  K  Q  W  H  I  N  E  S  W  T  C  O  Y
W  G  R  U  N  T  S  E  G  G  U  S  X  Z
```

Page 5: Position
The parrot squawked, "Look upstairs and you'll see!"
"Look upstairs," the parrot squawked, "and you'll see!"
"Look upstairs and you'll see!" the parrot squawked.

Page 6: Voice
Answers will vary.

Lesson 6 - Homophones, Homonyms, and Homographs

Page 1: I Know Homophones!

knight

bear

knot

mail

Page 2: Homophone Word List

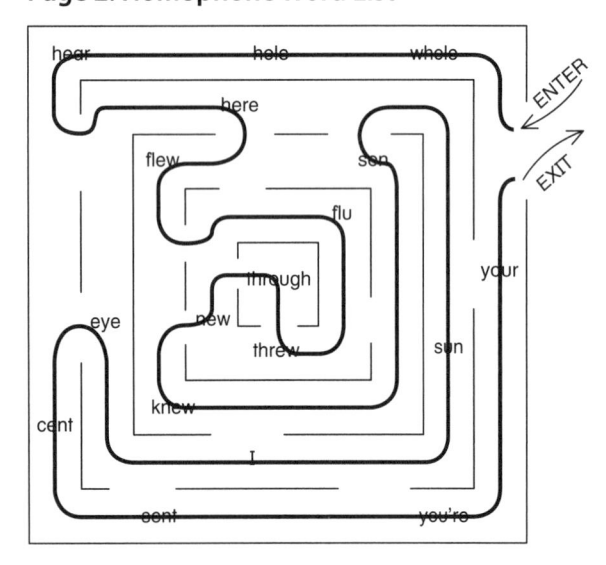

[maze diagram with homophone words: hear, hole, whole, here, flew, son, flu, through, new, threw, your, eye, sun, cent, know, I, sent, you're]

Page 3: I Know Homographs!

The ringmaster **wound** a rope around the pole.

The acrobat **does** amazing tricks on the high wire!

The clown jumped and **dove** into a bucket of water.

One clown played the **bass** guitar.

Look at the two fawns and three **does** in the pen.

See the trained **dove** fly through the hoop!

One of the lions has a **wound** on its paw.

The clown fished in a pond and caught a giant **bass**.

Page 4: Homonyms!

dance, pet

Page 5: Homonym Word List

Answers will vary.

Page 6: Fun with Words

Q: Why do bumblebees hum?

A: They don't **know** the words.

Q: Why is the bread full of **holes**?

A: Because it's **whole** wheat bread.

Lesson 7 - Five Paragraphs

Page 1: Five Paragraphs

Answers will vary.

Page 2: Kinds of Writing

1. Expository
2. Narrative
3. Persuasive
4. Narrative
5. Persuasive
6. Expository

Page 3: Transitions

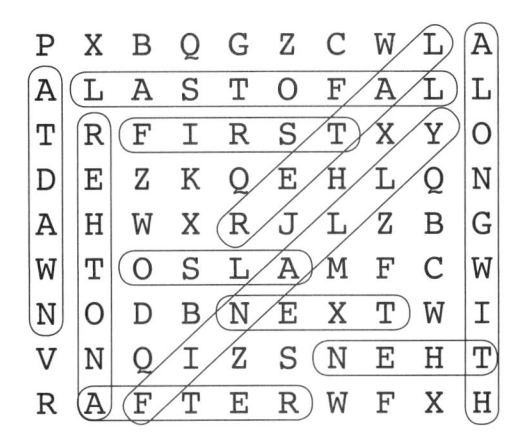

```
P  X  B  Q  G  Z  C  W  L  A
A  L  A  S  T  O  F  A  L  L
T  R  F  I  R  S  T  X  Y  O
D  E  Z  K  Q  E  H  L  Q  N
A  H  W  X  R  J  L  Z  B  G
W  T  O  S  L  A  M  F  C  W
N  O  D  B  N  E  X  T  W  I
V  N  Q  I  Z  S  N  E  H  T
R  A  F  T  E  R  W  F  X  H
```

Page 4: Introduction

#2: I ate **breakfast**.

#3: During practice, I stood next to the **shortstop**.

#4: At the game, I was **a batboy**.

Page 5: Body

Paragraph #2: First, I ate breakfast with all the players at the stadium.

Paragraph #3: After breakfast was finished, I went with the team to the field for practice.

Paragraph #4: At 3:00, the big game started.

Page 6: Closing

Circle the last paragraph.

Lesson 8 - Prefixes and Suffixes

Page 1: Prefix List

Answers will vary, but could be similar to these:

autobiography: story written by an author about himself
circumference: the measurement around a circle
dehydrate: to remove water
telescope: instrument used to see objects far away

Page 2: Root Words

-corn means *horn*: uni<u>corn</u>, bi<u>corn</u>, tri<u>corn</u>. *Drawings will vary.*

Note: *If your student recognizes the word "tricorn" as a three-cornered colonial or pirate hat, show him how the hat has three **horn-like** projections that give it its name.*

Page 3: Numerical Prefixes

pentagon: shape should have **five** sides
quadrilateral: shape should have **four** sides
octagon: shape should have **eight** sides

Page 4: Suffixes

Noun: soft + **ness** = softness
Verb: soft + **en** = soften
Adverb: loud + **ly** = loudly
Noun: loud + **ness** = loudness
Adjective: tight + **er** = tighter
Verb: tight + **en** = tighten
Adverb: quiet + **ly** = quietly
Adjective: quiet + **er** = quieter

Page 5: Prefixes and Suffixes

dependence — being influenced by something or someone
independence — freedom from another
transport — to take from one place to another
transportation — the act of carrying
kindness — a nice thing
unkindness — something mean or cruel

Page 6: Suffix List

Answers will vary, but could be similar to these:

in**let**:   small bay or cove along a river, sea, or lake coastline
magni**fy**:   to make larger
bi**ology**:   the study of living organisms
wool**en**:   made of wool

Lesson 9 - Compound Words

Page 1: Compound Words

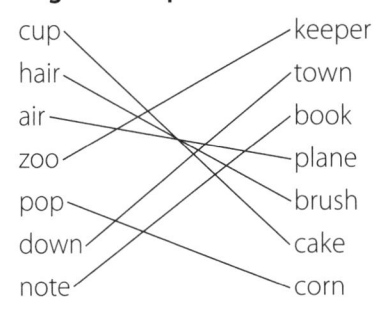

cup — cake
hair — brush
air — plane
zoo — keeper
pop — corn
down — town
note — book

Page 2: Hyphenated Compounds

son-in-law
know-it-all
year-end
self-editing
ten-year-old

Riddle: wrong

Page 3: Open Compounds

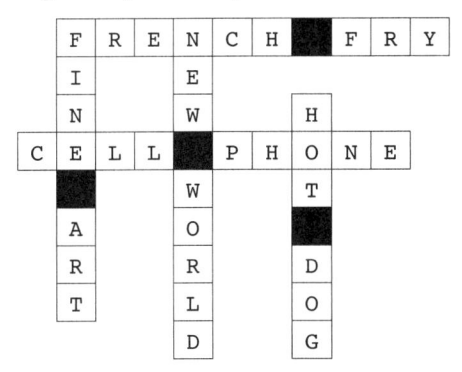

	F	R	E	N	C	H		F	R	Y
				I		E				
				N		W		H		
C	E	L	L		P	H	O	N	E	
				W				T		
	A			O						
	R			R			D			
	T			L			O			
				D			G			

Page 4: Compound Numbers

51: fifty-one   1/2: one-half
67: sixty-seven   22: twenty-two

Page 5: Plurals

mothers-in-law   toothbrushes
post offices   editors-in-chief
fingernails

Page 6: Adjectives

well-mannered   brand-new
well mannered   brand new

Lesson 10 - Synonyms and Antonyms

Page 1: Strong Words

walk = stroll
drink = slurp
look = peek
sleep = doze
sit = squat

Page 2: Strong Paragraphs

Answers will vary, but should be similar to these:

    The boa constrictor sleeps in his cage. This **reptile** likes to **rest** under the heat lamp. I want to get a **snake** like the one I saw **napping** in his **terrarium** at the Reptile Zoo.

Page 3: Synonyms

Answers will vary, but could be similar to these:

climb: scale, clamber, scramble, rise, increase
little: tiny, pint-size, small, young, miniature
hide: camouflage, cover, disguise, stash, stow away

Page 4: Antonyms

Answers will vary, but could be similar to these:

often: rarely, seldom, infrequently, occasionally
happy: sad, dejected, miserable, gloomy
safety: danger, risk, jeopardy, peril

Page 5: Humor

wet: dry
tall: short
lumpy: smooth

Page 6: Characters

Answers may vary, but should be similar to these.

Lex types **slowly**.
Lex wakes up **late**.
Lex likes sour **lemons**.

Gabi likes **sunny** weather. Lex likes **cloudy** weather.
Gabi likes **hot** weather. Lex likes **cold** weather.